ON
EASTER DAY
IN THE MORNING

Vicki Howie and Honor Ayres

Mary Magdalene has a wonderful friend called Jesus.

Everywhere Jesus goes, special things happen. There are picnics by the lake, and stories on the mountainside. Everyone stops work to listen to Jesus.

4

Children come running,
pit-pat, pit-pat, through the
streets and out of the town to be
blessed by Jesus.

Jesus always has time for
every one.

Everywhere Jesus goes, there are smiling faces.

Peter and John, the fishermen, pull in their fishing nets with a *heave ho*!

'Look how many fish Jesus has helped us catch!' they shout to each other.

A man who couldn't walk
rolls up his mat and steps out
left-right, left-right, through the
streets, and out of the town,
telling everyone he meets,
'Jesus has made me well!'

Whenever Jesus speaks, wonderful things happen. Storm clouds blow away and the sea becomes calm. Now his friends know that they are safe.

'Jesus is amazing!' they say. 'Even the wind and waves obey him.'

A man who was blind throws away his begging bowl and jumps up and down for joy.

'Jesus has made me see!' he tells everybody.

No wonder Mary and her friends love to follow Jesus!

But one day, some jealous men talk to each other, quietly, secretly.

'Everyone loves Jesus.'

'They all think he's special. They don't listen to us anymore.'

'Why don't we get rid of him?'

So, one night, when Jesus is praying among
the olive trees, soldiers march him away,
one-two, one-two, through the garden, into
the town and down the streets.

11

On Friday morning, a crowd of angry people shout, 'Kill him! Kill him!' and soldiers march Jesus away, one-two, one-two, through the gate leading out of the town, and up the hill, to die on a cross.

12

Poor Mary and her friends stand weeping, crying.
'Jesus is our special friend,' they say.

Now the sun hides its face. The ground shakes. Rocks break in two with a loud CRACK! And Jesus dies.

One frightened soldier looks on. He shakes his head.

'Oh no, oh no, Jesus really was special!' he says.

And Mary and her friends weep and hug each other.

That evening, a kind man says,
'I will take Jesus down from the cross.
I will bury Jesus in my cave.'
    Mary and her friends follow him,
slowly, sadly, down the hill, through a
gate and into a lovely garden.

Mary sits in the garden, crying, as friends place Jesus, kindly, gently, in the cave. They roll a big, heavy stone to close it, tight shut.

Then, slowly, sadly, Mary and her friends go home.

On Sunday, Mary creeps out of the house very early. No one else is awake yet. Even the sun isn't up on this Easter Day in the morning.

Softly, Mary tiptoes, tiptoes, along the streets, carrying some special herbs and spices. Then she meets her friends and together they walk through the gate leading out of the town, down the hill and into the lovely garden.

21

The sky glows pink as Mary and her friends walk, swish, swish, through the wet grass, closer and closer to the cave with the big, heavy stone.

Then they stop and stare.

Someone has rolled back the stone!

Someone has opened the cave!

'Someone has taken Jesus!' cries Mary, covering her eyes with her hands.

They run back into the town and Mary fetches
Peter and John.

'Come quickly!' Mary tells her friends. 'Come
and see!'

Peter and John run to the lovely garden. Peter and John see the empty cave and the empty grave clothes. They see that Jesus has gone! Then Peter and John run back home to tell the others.

Mary returns to the lovely garden and stays there, weeping, crying, as the sun climbs up over the hill. When Mary opens her eyes, she sees the glow, glow, of two shining angels, inside the cave where Jesus' body used to be.

'Don't cry, Mary,' they say, smiling. It's as if they knew a special secret.

Now someone is standing behind Mary.

'Why are you crying?' asks a kind voice.

Mary spins around.

'Mary,' says Jesus. 'It's me. Go and tell my friends that I am alive and they will see me soon.'

Mary runs as fast as she can, out of the garden, up the hill, through the gate leading into the town and along the streets.

Happy, happy, beats her heart. Mary goes to see her friends.

'I've something special to tell you,' says Mary.

'It's Jesus. He died but now he's alive! We'll see him soon.'

And Mary and her friends dance for joy. They want to tell everyone about Jesus and what happened on Easter Day in the morning.

29

Published in North America by: Liguori Publications
1 Liguori Drive, Liguori, MO 63057
Tel: 800-325-9521   Fax: 800-325-9526
www.liguori.org

ISBN: 978-0-7648-1999-5

First edition 2001, under the title 'Someone Very Special'
This new revised edition 2011

Copyright © 2011 Anno Domini Publishing
Book House, Orchard Mews, 18 High Street, Tring,
Herts HP23 5AH England
www.ad-publishing.com
Text copyright © 2001 Vicki Howie
Illustrations copyright © 2011 Honor Ayres

Publishing Director: Annette Reynolds
Art Director: Gerald Rogers
Pre-production Manager: Krystyna Kowalska Hewitt
Production Manager: John Laister

Printed and bound in Singapore